The Goal

Bobby Orr and the Most Famous Goal
in Stanley Cup History

ANDREW PODNIEKS

TRIUMPH
BOOKS
CHICAGO

Library of Congress Cataloging-in-Publication Data
Podnieks, Andrew.
    The goal : Bobby Orr and the most famous goal in Stanley Cup history / Andrew Podnieks.
        p. cm.
    ISBN 1-57243-570-4 (hard)
        1. Orr, Bobby, 1948– 2. Stanley Cup (Hockey) (1970) 3. Boston Bruins (Hockey team)—History.
    4. St. Louis Blues (Hockey team)—History. I. Title.

    GV848.5.O7P63 2003
    796.962'092—dc21
    [B]

                                                                                                        2003042614

This book is available in quantity at special discounts for your group or organization. For further information, contact:
Triumph Books
601 South LaSalle Street
Suite 500
Chicago, Illinois 60605
(312) 939-3330
Fax (312) 663-3557

Printed in the United States
ISBN 1-57243-570-4
Interior design by Wagner/Donovan Design

Photo Credits
The Brearley Collection: pp. 4, 14, 34.
Fred Keenan/Hockey Hall of Fame: pp. 6, 12, 20, 32.
Lorne Sandler/Hockey Hall of Fame: pg. 8.
Hockey Hall of Fame: pg. 26.
AP/Wide World Photos: pg. 16.
Al Ruelle: pp. 10, 18, 24, 36.
Corbis: pp. 22, 40.
Frank O'Brien/*Boston Globe*: pg. 28.
Ernie Cormier/Sports Action: pg. 30.
Canapress: pg. 38.

Contents

Foreword

The first time I saw Bobby Orr play was at Maple Leaf Gardens for the Memorial Cup back in the mid-sixties. I was a player/coach with the Bruins' farm team in Kingston, and we got beat out in our playoffs, so they asked me to watch this kid play in Toronto. Bobby had a groin injury and he could barely skate. Well, on his first shift, he skated over center ice and hit the goal post with a long slap shot. It was so obvious he was going to be great.

After Kingston, I was with Minneapolis for two years, and then I coached the Oklahoma City Blazers to a championship in 1965–66. That summer, Boston promoted me to head coach of the NHL team. I started in 1966–67, the same year Bobby did. He was the youngest player in the league and, at 34, I was the youngest coach in league history. I talked to Bobby a lot in those days, and we became friends. We did a lot of things together off the ice. We'd go fishing together, hunt birds together.

Because of Bobby and Phil Esposito and so many of the other players, we built those Bruins teams around offense. We could score more goals than anyone else in those days, and it was only a matter of time before the team became great. We just had to be patient and wait for the young guys to mature.

In our first year, we finished dead last and scored the fewest goals in the league. In our second year, we finished in third place and led the NHL in goals scored, but we lost in the first round of the playoffs. In 1968–69, we became the first team to score 300 goals in a season (303), and we went to the semifinals. And then in 1969–70, everything fell into place. Bobby won the Art Ross Trophy with 120 points, and Esposito finished second with 99. In the playoffs, we beat the Rangers in six games in the quarterfinals, and we swept Chicago four straight to make it to the finals against the West Division champions, St. Louis.

Our best games of that series were the first two in St. Louis when we won 6–1 and 6–2. Scotty Bowman tried to put a shadow on Bobby and it failed miserably, but you have to give credit to Scotty for trying something. We were just the better team, and Bobby was the best player in the world. In Game 3, we weren't quite as strong, but we won 4–1. I remember on the day of Game 4 thinking how much I didn't want to lose. We had won the first three games, and by then I knew for certain we were going to win the Stanley Cup—it was just a question of when. Everybody wanted it to be that day, and the team definitely didn't want to go back to St. Louis for a fifth game. On May 10, 1970, I found out that the clinching game was the most difficult to win, the game when the other team is facing elimination.

We didn't have our best game, and St. Louis played the way they should have. It was 3–3 going into overtime, but when you get to overtime, one bounce, one shot, and the game is over. Overtime doesn't necessarily tell you which team played the better game or which team was the better of the two. I put Bobby out to start the overtime because it was very unlikely that the Blues would get a top scoring chance with him out there.

As I said, we were always a very aggressive team in terms of offense, and I started Orr also in the hopes that he would set the tone for an offensive overtime. We started the Sanderson-Westfall-Carleton line (our checking line) up front because St. Louis started with its best line. Derek Sanderson was a fantastic offensive player, but he was on a team where we had to have a strong, checking centerman on one of the lines. Esposito and Fred Stanfield really didn't fit that mold, but Sanderson did, even though he was in a class with Esposito and Stanfield in terms of offense. He could have been a 40-goal scorer.

When Orr pinched on the winning play, the first thing I did was look to see what Ed Westfall was doing. That's what coaches do. You look to see if the players are doing the fundamentals. I saw Bobby go in, I had a good view of it, I saw Westfall come back to Bobby's position at the point the way he was supposed to, and I felt comfortable. Then, I started to look at the play.

Even if Bobby didn't get the puck and St. Louis had a breakaway, it was always worth the chance for him to pinch because maybe one in fifty times he wouldn't get the puck or get back in time. He was a fantastic, powerful skater. He was so much better than everyone, and it was almost a certainty that we'd win the overtime if he were on the ice.

Orr was really good at the give-and-go, especially with Sanderson. Bobby could headman the puck from behind his own net and get the puck at full speed before he hit his own blue line. And he had that explosive speed and creativity anywhere on the ice. There has never been a better give-and-go player than Bobby. But what often gets over-looked about that play was Derek's pass. He was a great playmaker, and that was a great pass he made to get the puck to Bobby.

As soon as the puck went in, I was stunned for a moment. Then, I leaped over the boards and jumped on somebody's back with everyone else. That night, I went out with the players after we left the Boston Garden. We had a party set up at the Colonial Hilton Hotel, and everyone was wildly ecstatic. It was Mother's Day. One reporter after the game asked me what I thought of the victory, and I said, "Everybody in this room can thank his mother for buying him his first pair of skates."

I know that a lot of the players and staff took a memento home from that game. I got Phil's sweater. But when we auctioned off memorabilia at the closing of the Garden in 1995 for the benefit of the Bruins alumni, I pulled that out of the closet and gave it up.

I would never have thought of this during the game, but after the fact I thought about how appropriate it was that Bobby scored the goal. It was such a spectacular goal for a defenseman, but in the previous four years he had ushered in a way to play the game that no one had ever played before (or since, for that matter). From the time we entered the league together in 1966 to the time he scored that goal, he changed the way the game was played. No one has ever played like that since. No one. ■

—**HARRY SINDEN**

I.

Matt Pavelich

"I was at the blue line," linesman Matt Pavelich stated excitedly. "I was the linesman behind Bobby Orr—that's a picture I'd like to have, but I can't find one with me in it."

Like referee Bruce Hood and linesman Ron Ego, Pavelich focused on his first concern during the overtime, which was to do his job properly. "It was a good play. We just wanted to make sure it was a good goal. Once the puck goes over the blue line, your job is to be aware of what's going on in case the referee asks for help." No such help was required, but Pavelich didn't leave the ice right away regardless. "We stayed on the ice until after the handshake, just to make sure nothing happened."

He and his colleagues stayed in the city longer than planned. "We wanted to go home, but all the roads were blocked. I called the wife and told her I couldn't get out and then we stayed and joined in the festivities. I had some friends in Boston, so we went to get a bite to eat and have a few drinks. It was the end of the season for us, too. In your mind, you've had a good season and you're glad it ended well."

Officials are just as aware and emotive as fans and players are. Even when they're on the ice and calling a game objectively, they know who's who, and they appreciate a good play or player as much as anyone does. Pavelich knew he was seeing someone special whenever he saw Orr play. "He was just such an exciting player."

Does he know what happened to the most prized souvenir from that day? "I'm not sure what happened to the puck. I got 'Boom Boom' Geoffrion's 51st puck and gave it to him—I have a picture of that—but I don't know what happened after Orr scored."

Pavelich's brother, Marty, made it to the NHL as a player, playing on four Stanley Cup winners with Detroit during the height of their power in the fifties. In 1987, Matt made it to the Hockey Hall of Fame, as a linesman, the first so honored after nine referees had been previously inducted over the years. He had been with the NHL for 31 years and had officiated more than 2,000 games, including 11 All-Star Games and 245 playoff games.

"In all the years I was in the league," he said proudly, "I was always in the Stanley Cup finals—not always in the final game when the Cup was presented, but always in the finals at some point." ■

2. Fred Keenan

Although Ray Lussier's photo has been the photo most frequently reproduced from this Stanley Cup–winning game, it was Fred Keenan's that won top honors from the Boston Press Photographers' Association at its annual contest at the end of the year. What made it better, they felt, was that Orr is still on the rise in Keenan's ultimate picture whereas in Lussier's he's on his way down.

Keenan's four-photo sequence ran the next day on the front page of the *Quincy Patriot Ledger*, a daily paper for a small chain of 29 towns in and around Boston. "When the game went into overtime, all the photographers moved to my end of the rink," Keenan said from his Cape Cod home in 1997, shortly before his death. Shooting with a Nikon F and without a flash, Keenan produced a sequence that seems to indicate that he knew a goal was going to be scored and he knew how it would be scored, so perfect are the moments in each frame. However, when editors and publishers from around the world wanted a photo of the Goal, they contacted Lussier at the *Herald American*, a much larger, better-known, and more widely distributed paper. Lussier was standing to Keenan's immediate right when they both caught Orr heading to the net.

Keenan began his life as a photographer taking pictures of destroyer escorts and launching craft from the Quincy, Massachusetts, shipyard during World War II. He had been declared 4-F for active service because of, ironically, weak eyes. After the war, he worked in commercial photography for a number of years at Alson Studios in Weymouth, Massachusetts, taking high school portraits and doing mostly studio work.

While there, he came to know the sister-in-law of the *Patriot Ledger*'s sports editor, Prescot Hobson, and it was she who recommended Keenan to Hobson when a position became available at the paper in early 1970. Ultimately, the great sequence didn't alter Keenan's life, and he continued shooting sports for the paper—the Red Sox, Celtics, and Bruins—until 1984, when he retired. ■

3. Ed Westfall

"One thing I've never, ever seen mentioned in all these years about that overtime," Ed Westfall began eagerly. "We had a team with the first line of Esposito, [Ken] Hodge, and [Wayne] Cashman, the highest-scoring line in the league. The second line was [John] McKenzie, Stanfield, and [John] Bucyk. And who does Harry Sinden send out to start the overtime? Sanderson, Carleton, and Westfall. I don't think anybody has ever asked Harry why he sent us out."

Perhaps Westfall unwittingly answered his own question when he started to talk about Orr pinching on the winning play. "When Bobby rushed up the ice, you covered for him—that's how we did it back then," No. 18 explained. As Orr pinched in the OT, "I was covering Orr's ass—covering the point where he should have been. As a matter of fact, I think I should have had an assist on the play."

He didn't get an assist, but he did get his name on the Stanley Cup for the first and only time in his 18-year career. "We went out to start the overtime with one thing in mind—all we could think about was winning. In overtime, you try to win as quickly as possible." Westfall was unequivocal about his team's killer instinct in such a situation. "We weren't thinking about trying to keep them from scoring—it was just gain control of the puck from the face-off and get the puck into the offensive zone and make things happen and win the game."

But like everyone else on the ice, his guess was as good as anyone's what Orr was going to do once he got control of the puck along the boards deep in the St. Louis end. "Any time Orr was on the ice, we had a chance for a goal. When he starts to move, things generally happen. I had no idea it was going to be a give-and-go. Watching how things unfolded, you just never knew it was going to be a goal."

Westfall and Ted Green were the senior players on the Bruins after Johnny Bucyk, so they had paid their dues with a team that routinely missed the playoffs during the sixties. That goal was sweet reward for a long wait. "The flying through the air wasn't a big deal," Westfall said. "The puck was already in the net—and that was a big deal. When [Noel] Picard caught Bobby's ankle, it was just a reaction to the fact that the game was over." ■

4. Derek Sanderson

"I made the kid famous!"

Maybe Derek Sanderson has watched the footage of the goal more than anyone, maybe he remembers the play with the clarity of a hockey player's genius, but, whatever the case, the fact is that not a nuance of that overtime has left his memory.

"I shot the puck wide and went around to the back of the net because if Bobby had fired the puck around I was going to try a wraparound. But when Bobby gave it to me it wasn't rocket science to realize he was going to the net. The key was getting it back to him because there was no one at the point. I had to make sure to get the puck over the one St. Louis stick and onto Bobby's. I was behind the net; it was a three-foot pass, and I'd have killed him if he missed it! It was perfect. When I passed it to him, I saw it get by [Glenn] Hall. The puck hit the net and then just spun around. The first thing I did was look at the referee to make sure it was all right. I thought there was no point in getting excited until it was official. I saw him [the referee] point, and it was all right, and I got to Bobby first."

Sanderson, perhaps more than anyone else on the ice at the time, worked well with Orr, the defenseman who was like a fourth forward. "We had done that many times in practice," he said of the quick give-and-go play. "I always played like that with Bobby—you knew when he gave you the puck that he'd take off. Bobby was always the one who made it happen. You know, what I was truly ecstatic about at that moment was that it was Bobby who got the goal. It

was very fitting. He had broken all sorts of records all year. He was the reason we were there, so it was fitting he got the goal.

"But we also had [Don] Awrey on the point, and he could skate with anyone in the league, so we were covered," he noted of a play fraught with gamble.

Sanderson also recalled the importance of coach Harry Sinden's philosophy. "Sinden always had a number of adages, and one of them was that most sudden deaths end quickly—a lucky bounce or bad break. Harry sent our line out because he wanted to get through the first minute, get a couple of whistles, protract things. He knew the longer it went, the better chance we had of winning it." That Sanderson's line started was almost a moot point to "Turk." "Our line had our share of goals. We had a lot of firepower, but it didn't matter who started—we had Orr out there."

Sanderson shed light both on Orr's kindness as a person and where the great No. 4 got some of his motivation: "Bobby would visit hospitals all the time. He'd know the patients by name—spina bifida kids whose greatest thrill was getting a fresh cast—and he'd come out of there pumped. He knew he was blessed with a gift." ■

5. Glenn Hall

From the second Bobby Orr decided to pinch in at the blue line until the moment the puck entered the net, no one else on the ice had the same vantage point that goalie Glenn Hall had from the confines of his crease. "I was trying to intercept the pass," he said of his attempt to poke-check the puck out of harm's way before Orr got to Sanderson's pass.

Hall is a Hall of Famer and arguably the greatest goalie the game has ever known, but this was one loss that didn't eat away at "Mr. Goalie." "We knew if we played to our potential and they played to theirs, the game would have been over in the first period," he admitted. "I apologize for not feeling badly that they beat us, but I don't. Geez, their coach must have been saying to them in the dressing room, 'Look at their lineup and look at ours—what are we doing in overtime with these guys?'"

While the Bruins players mobbed Orr for his heroics, the Blues players consoled their goalie and waited for the handshakes before leaving the ice. "After the goal, I was just focusing on going to the dressing room. The puck was in, there was nothing more we could do," Hall said, before adding, "I didn't feel bad it was the last game of the season; I was just happy I didn't have to put on that stinking equipment again for a while!"

Because Hall earned so many honors during his career, he can afford to be good-natured about his place in history for Orr's goal. "I told Bobby the game was over long before he landed," he joked about the flying finish to the game. Nonetheless, because Hall is front and center in the famous Ray Lussier photo, he sees it more often than any other happier image from his playing days. "I've signed that picture so many times . . . but it's still great. When I played at the All-Star Game in Boston [in 1971], every fan had a copy and I got my dollar for every autograph."

Hall is equally frank about the goal's place in Stanley Cup history. He said that it was a great goal by a great player, but within the context of the series it lacked the drama of, say, Pete Babando's double overtime goal in Game 7 of the 1950 Red Wings–Rangers finals to give Detroit the Cup. "I think overtime goals in Game 7 are the most exciting, but this was only Game 4," he noted. "Everyone knew these guys were going to win the series."

Hall quickly allocated a lofty place in hockey history to No. 4. "In my opinion, Gordie Howe was the greatest player of all time. But Orr was just a step away." ■

6. Ray Lussier

Ray Lussier's three-shot sequence of photographs of Orr's shot and midair celebration is one of the greatest series of images in the history of hockey, and it was captured under serendipitous circumstances, to say the least. Each photographer at the Boston Garden that day had been assigned a stool at the glass from which he had to work. Lussier had been in the east corner of the rink, but with the Bruins attacking in the west end in overtime, he headed there during the intermission after the third period.

Luckily, he found a free stool because one photographer had left his pew to get a beer! "I figured I'd stay there until the guy came back," Lussier explained years ago.

The other guy took too long in the lobby and didn't get back for the start of the OT. He heard the roar of the crowd, ran to his spot, and told Lussier to leave. With a great smile, Lussier happily obliged. "I told him, 'It's all yours; I've got what I need.'

"I never would have got the picture if that other photographer didn't go running off to get a beer." Out of respect, Lussier never revealed the name of that unlucky photographer.

Lussier was born in Lawrence, Massachusetts, a small French-Canadian area of that state. As a result, he grew up loving hockey, and it was his knowledge of the sport that helped him get that famous goal on film. "You have to know and love a sport to get peak action shots," he explained. "Anticipation is a lot in covering pro sports. Ice hockey . . . is a game of constant, quick action. Even when it's fast, you have to know how to wait for the sudden turns, switches, and scrambles."

He studied at the Franklin Institute of Photography in Boston in 1950 and worked for the *Boston Herald American* from 1964 until 1980. He later worked as a microfilm camera operator at the Northeast Document Conservation Center in Andover, Massachusetts, until his untimely death on March 19, 1991. He was just 59. ▪

7. Noel Picard

"If you're going to get scored on, I don't mind as long as it's Bobby Orr. To my mind, he was the greatest hockey player in the world," Noel Picard said with pride. Then, as an afterthought almost, "It was scored by No. 4 against No. 4."

If this game had been played today, Picard wouldn't have been around in overtime to augment Orr's celebratory dive—he would have been tossed from the game much earlier. In a first-period melee, a tussle between Don Awrey and Tim Ecclestone escalated to include Ray Fortin, John McKenzie, and Orr, at which point Picard came off the St. Louis bench to grab Orr and even things up. "I was afraid maybe Picard was being sent out to get him," coach Harry Sinden said after the game, though the situation didn't end up getting so out of hand.

Of course, Picard is almost as famous as Orr for the photos: his stick caught around Orr's ankle, helping to propel the Bruins defenseman off the ice and high into the Garden air. On the play, however, he was where he should have been. "I played right defense," he explained. "I couldn't go to him right away or else I'd lose my man. He had so much speed, by the time he was in front the puck was in. When I lifted him up, whoosh! And the puck came out of the net and he went flying!"

All these years later, all these famous photos later, Picard is more than a little philosophical about the play and equally proud to be a part of Stanley Cup history. "Those things happen so quickly. My God, he went six feet in the air! At the time, you think only that he's scored a goal. He scored on the short side, right in front of the goal. Then you see the pictures and you admire the play."

Picard's first recollections of that May day echo everyone else's: "It was hot, hot, hot. I lost 13 pounds that game. We had a good, family team, but with the team we played against, we were lucky to get into overtime with them. If we could have had one player to score goals, it would have made a difference. But Boston had Esposito, Hodge, Cashman, McKenzie, Bucyk, and Sanderson, so eventually they're going to score goals. We had good players, but they were all old."

Picard revealed a little-known fact about Scotty Bowman's blue line corps in that fourth game. "That game, we finished with three defensemen—Al Arbour, Jean-Guy [Talbot], and me—Barclay [Plager] and Bob [Plager] were hurt," and Bowman had dressed just five defensemen.

The celebration right after the goal was unusual in that it took place deep in the opponent's end. As a result, the Blues players had to hang closely around their goalie, Glenn Hall, and wait to shake hands in what wasn't much of a straight line but rather bunches of players. "You know you're done, so you skate around talking a little bit for a couple of minutes waiting to shake hands," Picard said. "The time goes by quickly. That's part of life." ∎

8. Al Ruelle

During the game, photographer Al Ruelle didn't stay put in one place. He wandered around with his camera and took a variety of shots. But once overtime began, he focused on the St. Louis end. After all, Ruelle reasoned, if the Blues had won in overtime, the goal would have no historic significance save to extend the series to a fifth game. If Boston scored, the Cup belonged to the Bruins for the first time since 1941.

Ruelle moved up to the front row of the balcony, "sitting in baskets, almost hovering over the ice," he recalled of his walk up during the intermission before the overtime. As soon as Orr scored, Ruelle hurried down onto the ice to take more pictures, where "fans roared onto the ice as never before." From there, he quickly moved into the Bruins' dressing room.

Incredibly, this sequence of three photographs was never published as a group in the days that followed the Boston Stanley Cup victory. Ruelle suffered the same fate as Fred Keenan: "The Lussier shot came out and then everyone wanted that and no other, so all others were quickly forgotten," he stated flatly. Nonetheless, this three-shot is a phenomenal addition to the collection of images of the goal that won Boston the 1970 Stanley Cup. ■

9. Wayne Carleton

"I had a front-row seat for the goal. I was right behind him, about 10 feet in front of the net. If he'd have missed it, I was right there."

Wayne Carleton himself was a little surprised that his line started the overtime—that is, until he heard the explanation right from the horse's mouth. "Harry [coach Sinden] told me when I asked him why he started our line that it was easy for him to do because we had been the best line on our team for the last three games. And he was right, even though we didn't have the superstars. Not many coaches would have done that."

So there he was, out on the ice just feet away from the defining moment of Orr's career. "It was a special goal, and the right guy got it," Carleton said. "If I'd have scored, no one would have remembered." He recalled the play in words as simple but effective as Orr's move: "I remember hitting big Picard and the puck came around the corner and then it was over. Bobby came across from Hall's left side and put it between his legs. As he's landing on the ice, I have my stick in the air. I was the first to congratulate him."

That Carleton was with the team at all was a stunning reversal of fortune from opening night of the season. He began the year with Toronto, the team that Boston had humiliated in the previous spring's playoffs by scores of 10–0, 7–0, 4–3, and 3–2. Carleton had played seven games with the Leafs and six more in the minors with Phoenix of the WHL and just didn't seem to be a part of the Leafs' long-term plans. On December 10, 1969, Boston traded Jim

Harrison to Toronto to get Carleton, a trade that changed Carleton's life.

"I always thank Uncle Miltie [Boston general manager Milt Schmidt] for getting me," Carleton said good-naturedly. "When I was in Toronto, I was not their favorite son, but as time passes you realize the irony, and I'm very grateful for the Leafs letting me play in Boston. That game was a great highlight of my career. Any time you're on the ice when your team wins the Stanley Cup, it's a very special moment."

Like everyone else on the Bruins, Carleton dismissed the flying dive as important to the team at the time. "That [flying through the air] had nothing to do with how he scored. It was just the impression that we had won the Stanley Cup that was important. Bobby was just a great player. He had great anticipation and instinct, and all you had to do was based on what his situation was.

"The nice part about that team was that there was no selfishness. That season went by really quickly, and with that goal we won the Stanley Cup!" ■

10. Red Berenson

"I don't remember anything about the game except the last goal," Red Berenson began in telling his version of the goal. "Actually, Orr poked the puck past me. I was attacking him on the point, and he passed by me and went to the net. If I had got past him, I would have had a breakaway." He didn't.

"Talbot and I wore the same white helmets, but that's him behind the net," he continued. "I turned around; I couldn't catch him, but I saw the whole thing. I knew when his stick went in the air and Pic lifted him up that the series was over. It was a good goal—he was a player who was truly great."

So great, in fact, that Orr intimidated his opponents without ever doing anything. "It was confusing," Berenson related, "because Bowman used either [Jim] Roberts or [Terry] Crisp, whoever was on the ice, to shadow Orr. But I remember one time Crispie had the puck and passed it right to Orr and started chasing him! Sometimes they were so focused on trying to stop him they couldn't do anything else."

Such was the impact Orr had on opponents. "We had tried to shut him down and minimize his impact, but it was no surprise it was he who scored."

Berenson, though, was not as convinced as some of his teammates that the Bruins were shoo-ins to win the series. "We had played well, and I was having a good game. We were down three games to none, but our team had lots of energy and we still felt that if we could win the game, we would be going home and maybe could fight our way back into the series.

"We were the underdogs, the expansion team in the finals. We had one or two guys who had 20 goals, and they had six or seven. We didn't have anyone in the superstar category of player, and they were a great team. No doubt about it." ■

II. Don Awrey

Even all these years later, every Bruins player on the ice at the time of the goal still exudes a remarkable confidence in that team's ability to win. "I think St. Louis realized we were the better team—we just had so much talent that year," Don Awrey said. He would know—his defense partner was No. 4.

"Going into OT, we knew all we had to do was score one goal to win the Cup. It wasn't a critical play in that if they came down the ice and scored, we still had three games left to win the Cup." Nonetheless, Awrey reacted with due caution as he saw Orr pinch at the blue line. "The way Bobby used to play, I always had one foot ready to go back when I saw him move up. On that play, I was just going to hold my position on the point until something happened or didn't happen."

It happened all right. "That play opened up and allowed him to go to the net, but I don't even know if Bobby was thinking of the give-and-go when he put the puck to Derek in the corner, and I don't know if that's what Derek was thinking, either."

Indeed, Awrey played his position not thinking about the other team but rather in deference to his improvisational partner, Orr, who controlled every game he played. "I complemented him because he felt free to go, and he sure complemented me. You could never guess what he was going to do; you could never figure out what his next move was," Awrey said with continued awe. If his own teammates were left guessing, imagine how Orr's

opponents must have felt every time he came up ice with the puck.

Like everyone else on the team, it was the red goal light on the play that counted to Awrey, not the flying celebration. "The dive wasn't a big deal until the photo came out," Awrey offered. "At the time, the only thing I thought was about the goal being scored. I don't think the photo would have become as famous if I had scored the goal!"

12. Tim Ecclestone

"I can still remember the play vividly," Tim Ecclestone began, "the puck coming to Orr at the point, him coming down the boards and then heading to the net.

"If you look at the video replay," Ecclestone repeated with clarity, "there's a No. 14 that skates through the frame quickly. I was on the right side, and when I saw Orr pinch I skated toward the goal. I couldn't do much. I was on the other side to where Orr was, so all I was trying to do was stop anyone from Boston's left side—I couldn't do much about Orr. I had a pretty good look at the goal, though."

Like any journeyman who makes it to the NHL, Ecclestone appreciated what he had. He may not have been the most talented player in the game, but he made it to the big tent longer than most. For him, the glass was always half full. "Looking back, I was fortunate enough to play in Bobby Orr's prime. He was the best. He was the only player who could singlehandedly take control of a game.

"Later, I was thinking that there are Hall of Famers who have never been to the Stanley Cup finals, and here I was at 21 or 22 and had been there three times. We had the greatest coach of all time, and we were just a bunch of guys. We weren't necessarily the second-best team in the league, but we went to the Stanley Cup finals three years in a row. We never won a game, but every one was close. We played Montreal [in 1968] and lost three times by one goal."

Ultimately, the difference was the potent attack of those Original Six teams in the East Division that could come up with an important goal whenever one was needed.

"We just couldn't compete offensively with Montreal or Boston," Ecclestone acknowledged.

In defeat, as the players grouped around Glenn Hall, Ecclestone was philosophical if not perfunctory as the Bruins mobbed Orr. "You're down. You're on the losing side. You shake hands, and you get out of there. They were going to celebrate, and we were going home." ∎

13. Ron Ego

The life of referees and linesmen is hardly glamorous. "We used to get dressed in the hotel above the train station and put on a coat and carry our skates down to the dressing room at the Garden," Ron Ego explained, before adding, "Then we'd go back to the hotel to shower." Ah, the old Boston Garden. It was a character in a novel, a world unto itself.

On the afternoon of May 10, 1970, the officials' dressing room had a special visitor—the Stanley Cup. In the days before the glitz and white gloves and ceremony of bringing the Cup out to center ice, the officials used to travel with the Cup or, alternatively, the Hockey Hall of Fame's curator, Lefty Reid, would take it from city to city and leave it with the referee and linesmen.

The final game of the 1969–70 season was replete with memory for Ego. "I refereed through junior with him," he recalled of the parallel between Orr's career and his own. This finals game was also his last after four years as a linesman. The next fall, he became a referee.

"It was easier to appreciate him [Orr] when I wasn't on the ice. When you're on the ice, you're focusing on the puck, so it's always kind of hard to appreciate a play until after the fact. When the puck went in, I was very happy because it was a good, clean goal. Once I knew that, then I could admire it. Our job as front linesman is to focus on the puck."

Ego made a unique observation about the play: "It was such an unusual goal. You never thought he'd score from that angle, but he could do anything. I'd say one in ten times the puck would go in from where he shot it. But I still say he was one of the best of all time."

Usually, as soon as the game ends fair and square, the officials hustle off the ice anonymously and get on with their lives. Not this crew, not this day. "We stayed at the penalty box for a while after the goal," Ego said. "This game was the highlight of my career. Any time you work in the Stanley Cup finals, it's a big game, the dream of any official, just like the players.

"We were supposed to catch a 7:00 flight that night— we got home Tuesday! We partied with the people in Boston. The town was pretty happy!" ■

14. Ernie Cormier

Ernie Cormier is living testament to the difficulty of getting a seat to a game at the Boston Garden during the height of the Bruins' power. He was at the finals, sitting in a section known as the Gallery Gods, a seat he had had from the late fifties until 1977. To get a ticket, you had to know one of the section leaders who'd sell you a seat to the next game. Cormier got to know one and managed to get three seats—one for himself, one for his wife, and one for a friend—to Game 4.

The Gallery Gods were located in the second balcony. The first row of seats was great, but behind that row the view was less optimal because everyone else stood, thus obscuring the near boards. "They were the highest seats in the building, but they gave you a tremendous overview," Cormier recalled.

Cormier remembered the weather first. "It was an exceptionally warm day, and the Boston Garden had no air-conditioning," said Cormier, who was 32 at the time and a member of Local 25 of the Boston Teamsters. Like many a fan, he brought his camera to the game. The Bruins hadn't won the Stanley Cup since 1941, and this day promised great hope. During the course of the game, he took only a few pictures, but when overtime started he readied his camera because history seemed so close as to be almost tactile, predictable.

"What happened was this," he explained of his place in Bruins history. "I saw Bobby Orr keep the puck in the zone. He started skating toward the direction of the net, not in a straight line but in that direction, and I thought,

'Wow! Something might happen.' So I put the camera up to my face and centered it on the net, and the instant the red light went on I hit the shutter."

His timing was utterly perfect, though he never studied photography or practiced the art of split-second picture taking. "I was not a trained photographer, but I did play shinny in my youth. As a result, I had the ability to anticipate the situation." How well he had anticipated he didn't know for quite some time. Although pandemonium broke out in the building, he didn't remain in the Garden for too long after the goal. "I wanted to hang around and savor the moment, but my friend wanted to get along, and we always rode in together, so we left right after the presentation of the Cup."

When he got home, life continued as normal for Cormier, and his camera remained on his shelf. "Because developing was expensive, I had to be selective in how many pictures I took, and I didn't get the film developed right away. I was just married and had a kid on the way."

Eventually, though, he took his Ektachrome slide film to be processed, and when he saw the result, he was amazed. "When I saw the picture, I thought this was something special and I put it beside the famous Ray Lussier shot. If you look at where the puck is in the two pictures, we each took our picture in almost the exact same instant but from opposite sides of the building." The coincidence was remarkable, and the shots, taken for different reasons, captured the same pithy moment in hockey history, yet each is a story in itself. ■

15. Bobby Orr

The hero explained the play: "The puck came around the boards . . . but I knocked it back in the corner to Derek. . . . If it had gone by me, it's a two-on-one. So I got a little lucky there, but Derek gave me a great pass and when I got the pass I was moving across. As I skated across, Glenn had to move across the crease and had to open his pads a little. It's very difficult for a goaltender to move across and keep his legs closed. I was really just trying to get the puck on net, and I did. As I went across, Glenn's legs opened. I looked back, and I saw it go in, so I jumped. Then Noel Picard helped a little by lifting his stick under my skate."

Blues coach Scotty Bowman pacified all doubters as to the wisdom of Orr pinching in from the blue line during the first minute of an overtime game. "Sure it was a gamble for him, but the kid would have gotten back on time if he hadn't put the puck in the net. Believe me, he would have been back to cover up."

Mother Orr wasn't at the Boston Garden that afternoon—she didn't like to watch her son play. "My dad was there," Orr noted. "We were staying at the Colonial in Lynnfield. The whole team. The morning after the game, I met my dad for breakfast, and that was the first time I saw that picture of me flying through the air."

Orr, though, deflected the personal fame attached to the dive. "If I hadn't scored the overtime goal," he pointed out, "the thrill would have been the same. A dream was fulfilled."

This was the Bruins' first overtime win in the playoffs since March 27, 1958, when Jerry Toppazzini beat the Rangers 4–3 at Madison Square Garden. Of course, the Bruins hadn't won the Cup since 1941, a year Orr had been made aware of by local media from the first day he arrived in Beantown and was called the Second Coming by one and all in the city. Ending the B's drought only added to his own satisfaction. "It was special. We hadn't won the Cup in all those years. Growing up in Canada, lying in bed at night, that was something I'd dreamed about. There I was, following Chief [Johnny Bucyk] around the ice with him hoisting the Cup over his head. It was cool."

Holding and hugging the Cup, drinking from the bowl and admiring it, were made all the more cool that year because it was the last year that the original bowl of the Stanley Cup was in circulation. In the summer, it was retired to the Hockey Hall of Fame and a new one put in place. The original bowl had been through plenty since being awarded for the first time in 1893, and the Hall feared for its longevity. Today, it sits comfortably inside the vault room at the Hockey Hall of Fame in downtown Toronto.

Orr was named winner of the Conn Smythe Trophy the next day by vote of the NHL Board of Governors. The NHL soon changed the rules so that the winner would be named immediately after the final game and presented with the trophy on ice as a prelude to the Stanley Cup. Orr became the first man to win four major trophies in a season—Hart, Art Ross, Norris, and Conn Smythe—a feat that has yet to be replicated. He also set an NHL record for most goals (nine) and points (20) by a defenseman in one playoff year.

16. Bruce Hood

A goal isn't a goal until the referee says it is. Bruce Hood saw the play unfold from his spot on the end red line and declared Orr's goal good. "My claim to fame is that you can see about six inches of my hand and arm in the corner of the famous picture," he quipped of his place in hockey history. "I'm actually standing to the left of the net facing the net. Obviously, by the time he was flying through the air the goal had been scored. I saw it and thought, 'Oh, it's over.' It happened so quickly, but there's so much drama in that moment. When you go into overtime, every play is climactic because one goal and the game is over."

At that point, the officials were no longer needed. "We went off the ice pretty quickly—our job was over, the game was over, and the celebration began that we weren't really a part of." Hood, however, was so caught up in the game's conclusion that he forgot to perform his final on-ice duty of the season. "I was in the dressing room," he remembered, "and I realized I never did go to the penalty box to give the score! The truth of the matter is that the referees don't need to announce the goals, but it's just a part of the tradition of the game."

An incongruous element to the afternoon of May 10, 1970, was the weather, and Hood, like everyone else that day, recalled it vividly the way only heat can summon the senses. "I remember walking around Boston in the afternoon, and it was so warm, so hot, and there I was, getting ready for my first Stanley Cup finals game."

After the drop of the puck, he forgot the heat and went to work. "The game was basically as I anticipated it would be—good, steady flow, good solid checking by both teams, but nothing outstanding except that one team could win the Stanley Cup, so you knew there wouldn't be any foolishness. The development of the [winning] play was routine: moving up ice, moving into the corner, and scoring. I can't remember what it was exactly about the play, but it was much different in my mind to what actually happened when I watched it again on video."

But for a Bruce Hood call in the second period, Orr's goal would never have been scored. With St. Louis ahead 3–2, Hood disallowed a goal by Phil Esposito at 7:30 of the period on the grounds that Espo had deflected the puck with a high stick. Had it counted, Johnny Bucyk's goal in the third would have been the winner, and overtime would never have been played. "It [the disallowed goal] was nothing significant, pretty routine," Hood said of his call that was long forgotten at the 40-second mark of overtime.

A goal isn't a goal until the referee says it is. ■

17. Jean-Guy Talbot

"As long as it's Bobby Orr, that's OK—if it would have been a fourth-line guy, I'd feel kind of bad, but not if it's Bobby Orr. It was an honor to be on the ice with him," said Jean-Guy Talbot. That's the influence Orr had on the game. Players tried their hardest against him and did what they could to beat him or slow him down, but at the end of the day, they knew they were in the presence of true, unstoppable greatness.

Talbot won seven Stanley Cups with Montreal and was near the end of a long and distinguished career as a member of the Blues. "It never mattered who we played with on defense. Sometimes I played with Picard, sometimes with Al Arbour—it didn't matter as long as I played."

It was Talbot's touch of the puck that began the final play of the 1969–70 season. "I was behind the net with another player, so I had a very good view of the goal," he related with a chuckle. "I got the puck around the boards and Larry Keenan was watching the point, but he missed the puck and Orr moved right in." From that moment, Talbot sensed the danger.

"When Orr has the puck at the blue line, you expect him to walk right in. He doesn't score every game, but you expect him to do that." On this play, he did, indeed, score, and although the drama of the moment was high, the outcome was, in Talbot's mind, predetermined. "We were lucky to make the finals," he admitted, referring to the postexpansion setup of 1967, which saw the Original Six in one division (East) and the new teams in another (West) to ensure one from each section made it to the finals. "We couldn't be disappointed with the results. We tried, but we weren't disappointed. We made the finals three times in a row, but we didn't win a game." The Blues were seventh best, in a sense.

And he admits more. "Even if we won [Game 4], that was just one game. We still would have lost the series. With expansion, we didn't have the team to beat those guys." ■

18. Larry Keenan

Larry Keenan was no superstar in the NHL, but he was a member of the Blues in each of the three seasons the team went to the finals (1968, '69, and '70). He was no great scorer, either, but he played his best hockey in the post-season. "I was always fortunate enough to play well in the playoffs," he concurred. "In those three years, I had 15 goals and 6 were game winners."

Keenan got the Blues to the finals with a game- and series-winning goal against Pittsburgh in the division finals, and in this Game 4 it was his goal 19 seconds into the third period that gave the Blues a 3–2 lead that led to the over-time. It was the last lead the Blues enjoyed in the series. His backhander went high off Gerry Cheevers' arm and into the top corner, and in the fourth period, it was his gamble that led to Orr's heroics.

"Our defenseman [Jean-Guy Talbot] fired the puck around the boards, and I wanted to tip it by Orr. Red Berenson was breaking down the middle as soon as he saw Orr pinch, so if I got it out he would have had a breakaway and might have won the game for us. But, the puck didn't stay low and instead it went high and hit Orr and he got it into the corner. He gambled and I gambled, but I thought it was certainly worth it. It was going to be either a good play or bad, but if I didn't know the outcome, I'd do the same thing again.

"Orr was one of the few guys in the league who would gamble on that play, but a player can gamble a lot more when he's up three games to none," Keenan opined.

Nonetheless, he quipped, "I tell people that I got beaten by the best—that's what it took to beat me!"

Like all other players on both teams, he appreciated the goal for who scored it rather than the circumstances under which it was scored. "Our guys didn't make a big deal of it. From my perspective, if it was a sudden death of the seventh game it would have been a dramatic goal, but all it did was give them a four-game sweep. It wasn't a spectacular win, but it was a spectacular photograph."

Unlike some of his teammates, Keenan felt the loss, regardless of its inevitability. "Even though you're down three games to none and you know they're the better team, you still have an unhappy feeling watching them celebrate," he admitted.

Following the handshakes, the Blues skated off the ice for the final time of the year, and Keenan grew wistful at the close of the day. "In the dressing room, we stuck around a little longer, and on the flight home we talked about the good things and all that we had accomplished." ■

19. Gerry Cheevers

"When he scored, I threw my stick high in the air and started to skate to the other end. But when I got to the top of the circle in my end, I thought I might like to keep that stick, so I went back to get it. Luckily for me, it was balancing on the top of the glass and fell back onto my side! So I got it and skated down to the other end," said Bruins goaltender Gerry Cheevers.

It was an atypical way for a goalie to celebrate victory, and probably never before or since has a goalie skated so far to join the hugs. Usually in a Cup-clinching game, time winds down in the goalie's end, the final bell goes, and the players mob the masked man who is, by definition, the center of attention. But not with Orr on the ice. He was the focus of all the jubilation.

St. Louis coach Scotty Bowman said after the game that he thought Cheevers should have won the Conn Smythe Trophy (which, in those days, wasn't presented until the day after the Cup-winning game). "It was nice of Scotty to say that, but no question Bobby was the MVP," Cheevers demurred.

The scar-masked goalie, however, is like Sanderson in his willingness to take some credit for Orr's heroics in overtime, albeit playfully. "If it wasn't for me, Bobby never would have scored that goal," he said, tongue in cheek. "I let in three bad goals during the game. I think I could have had a couple of them. All I had to do was stop one of them and we'd have won [in regulation]."

Truth be told, though, Cheevers also made a fantastic save in the third when he stopped Larry Keenan in close to preserve the tie and force overtime. "Actually, I remember the play because Keenan and I were at St. Mike's together," he related of their junior days in Toronto. "It was a strange play. I was falling one way, and I threw my hand back the other way and caught the puck in my glove."

In some ways, Cheesie had the best seat in the house to see the goal. "As soon as he pinched, I thought, 'Good, we have a chance to win.'" After he joined in the on-ice festivities, he headed to the dressing room to be with his dad and a couple of his dad's friends.

Players' fathers Joe Cheevers, Doug Orr, and Harold Sanderson were all, at various times, carted off by the players to the showers for a celebratory soaking. ■

Postscript: the Puck

Perhaps it is the stuff of legend, perhaps an unknown truth, but at least one account has it that during the mob scene on the ice after Orr's goal, trainer Frosty Forristall managed to scoop the puck from the St. Louis net. As the story goes, he taped it and recorded the pertinent information, and shortly before his death in June 1995 he gave the puck to a friend, who tried to auction it off in late 2002.

There are two contradictions to this hypothesis, though. Frosty, Eddie Johnston, Gary Doak, and Bobby Orr—all unmarried—lived together in a house in Boston. Frosty would have known of the puck's importance to Orr and likely wouldn't have kept his owning it a secret from Orr, who likely would have wanted it for himself, of course.

Second, Frosty worked under head trainer Dan Canney, and Canney remembers Forristall heading into the dressing room quickly after the game ended. "I got the sticks into the room right away," Canney recalls, "and I think Frosty went in even sooner to get the video [the trainers taped all games for scouting and practice purposes]."

However, *The Hockey News* of June 1970, which featured stories on the finals, supports the myth at Canney's expense. In its game report, it states: "Youngsters tried to grab Orr's stick before it was rescued by a Boston trainer." Curiouser and curiouser.

Canney does recall that to mollify one fan who was almost on the Bruins players' bench, he gave the man a photographer's stool from the end of the Boston bench. In the playoffs, when teams could dress an extra man, the benches became too short, so the stool was used for the extra player. Canney also revealed that just a short time after the game he noticed that the goal net that Orr scored into was missing! "I don't know how they got it out of there," Canney said, "but somewhere in Boston a guy's got that net in his basement or garage."

It was Canney who hired Forristall back in 1963. Canney knew Frosty's mother, who sold concessions at the Garden, and she asked him about a job for her son who was just coming out of the Marine Corps. Forristall had been called Snowman in his early days because he looked like a snowman in goal when he played for the high school hockey team back in North Quincy. Down through the years the name changed slightly to Frosty, though nothing could be further from the truth as far as his personality. "He was always smiling," Canney remembers.

Canney taught Frosty about sharpening skates, handling players' sticks, picking up equipment from the airport, and even a few medical tricks of the trade. On the road, they roomed together, and they were like brothers as much as colleagues.

Frosty was trainer for Team Canada during the historic 1972 Summit Series against the Soviet Union, and he later was trainer for the Toronto Blue Jays and Tampa Bay Lightning. He died of a brain tumor at age 52. Although he never smoked a day in his life, he had two black lungs, the result of secondhand smoke. Only he knew for certain whether he got the puck, though Orr believes he himself has it at home. "It was a madhouse on the ice after I scored and I didn't get a chance to get the puck. . . . I was given a plaque with the puck by [the Bruins owners]. The plaque says 'Overtime Goal' and has all the details on it."

Orr thinks he has it; Forristall's friend thinks he has it. The truth might never be known. "I've heard of one or two of the pucks floating around through the years," Orr acknowledged. ■

Game Summary

St. Louis 3 at Boston 4 (OT)			May 10, 1970, Boston Garden		
BOSTON BRUINS			**ST. LOUIS BLUES**		
Number	Position	Player	Number	Position	Player
1	G	Gerry Cheevers	1	G	Glenn Hall
4	D	Bobby Orr	2	D	Ray Fortin
7	F	Phil Esposito	4	D	Noel Picard
8	F	Ken Hodge	5	D	Bob Plager
9	F	John Bucyk	6	F	Jim Roberts
10	D	Rick Smith	7	F	Red Berenson
11	F	Wayne Carleton	8	D	Barclay Plager
12	F	Wayne Cashman	9	F	Frank St. Marseille
16	F	Derek Sanderson	10	F	Phil Goyette
17	F	Fred Stanfield	11	F	Gary Sabourin
18	F	Ed Westfall	12	F	Terry Crisp
19	F	John McKenzie	14	F	Tim Ecclestone
20	D	Dallas Smith	15	F	Bill McCreary
22	F	Jim Lorentz	17	D	Jean-Guy Talbot
24	D	Bill Speer	18	F	Larry Keenan
25	D	Gary Doak	19	F	Andre Boudrias
26	D	Don Awrey	20	F	Ab McDonald
29	F	Don Marcotte	22	F	Terry Gray
Coach		Harry Sinden	Coach		Scotty Bowman

Shots on Goal					
	1ST PERIOD	2ND PERIOD	3RD PERIOD	OT	TOTAL
St. Louis	14	7	10	0	**31**
Boston	10	8	13	1	**32**

FIRST PERIOD

1. Boston, R. Smith (Sanderson)   5:28
2. St. Louis, Berenson (Bob Plager, Ecclestone)   19:17

Penalties: Boston, Sanderson (0:40); St. Louis, Ecclestone, Fortin, Picard and Boston, McKenzie, Orr (4:39); Boston, McKenzie (7:14); St. Louis, Picard (8:07); Boston, Stanfield (12:58); Boston, Awrey (16:04); St. Louis, Boudrias and Boston, Stanfield (18:36)

SECOND PERIOD

3. St. Louis, Sabourin (St. Marseille)   3:22
4. Boston, Esposito (Hodge)   14:22

Penalties: Boston, Sanderson (4:21); St. Louis, Berenson (6:32); Boston, McKenzie (11:55); Boston, D. Smith (18:52)

THIRD PERIOD

5. St. Louis, Keenan (Goyette, Roberts)   0:19
6. Boston, Bucyk (McKenzie, R. Smith)   13:28

Penalties: Boston, Esposito and St. Louis, Fortin (6:15); St. Louis, Bob Plager (8:25)

OVERTIME

7. Boston, Orr (Sanderson)   0:40

Penalties: none

Attendance	14,835
Referee	Bruce Hood
Linesmen	Ron Ego and Matt Pavelich

Acknowledgments

The author would like to thank the many people who have assisted with collecting these images and stories in one way or another to make this book possible. Thanks to Phil Pritchard, Tyler Wolosewich, Craig Campbell, Darren Boyko, Izak Westgate, Steve Poirier, Jeffrey Fletcher, Anthony Fusco, Peter Jagla, Marilyn Robbins, and Margaret Lockhart at the Hockey Hall of Fame. Thanks to the Bostonian Society, Kathleen Cable, Tina Poitras, Andrea Gordon, Donald Bowden, Michael Contant, Les Dunbar, Chuck at nhlmvp7o, Randall Lussier, Linda Beeler, and of course, the photographers lucky enough to have been in the building and skillful enough to have captured the goal. Thanks to Steve Babineau, Ernie Cormier, Carl Lavigne, Dan Canney, Lois Sinatra, Paul Patskou, and Barbara Keenan. And a special thanks to the Brearleys for restoring Ray Lussier's three-shot to its original glory. And last, thanks to Harry Sinden and the players for their time and enthusiasm for talking about the goal and playing the game with a passion that cannot be described. ■